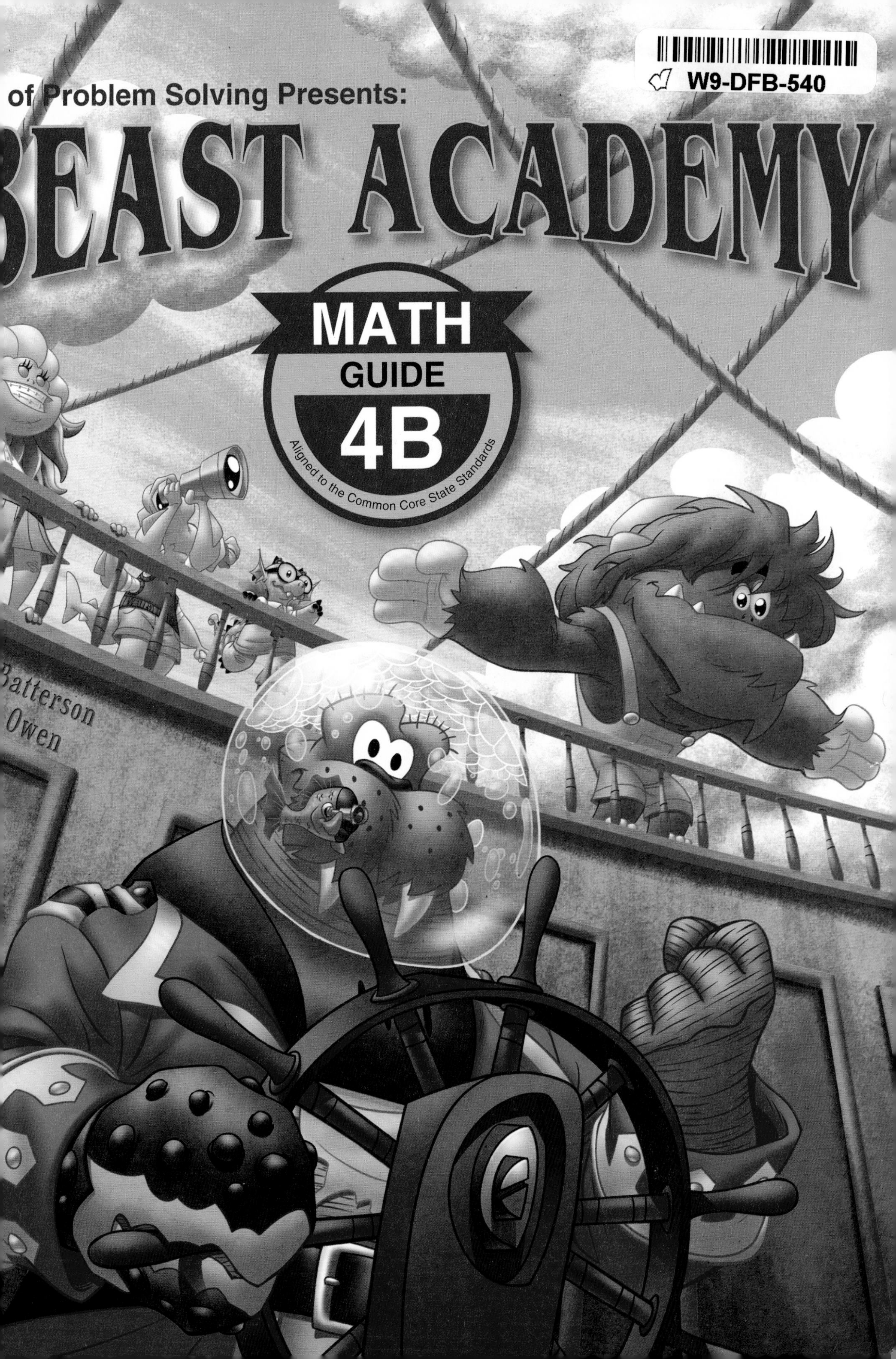

of Problem Solving Presents:

BEAST ACADEMY

MATH
GUIDE
4B

Aligned to the Common Core State Standards

Batterson
Owen

Published by: AoPS Incorporated
                     P.O. Box 2185
                     Alpine, CA 91903-2185
                     (619) 659-1612
                     info@BeastAcademy.com

ISBN: 978-1-934124-52-9

Beast Academy is a registered
trademark of AoPS Incorporated.

Written by Jason Batterson
Illustrated by Erich Owen
Colored by Greta Selman
Cover Design by Lisa T. Phan

Visit the Beast Academy website at www.BeastAcademy.com.
Visit the Art of Problem Solving website at www.artofproblemsolving.com.
Printed in the United States of America.
First Printing 2014.

Become a Math Beast!
For additional books,
printables, and more, visit
www.BeastAcademy.com

This is Guide 4B in a four-book series for fourth grade:

Guide 4A
Chapter 1: Shapes
Chapter 2: Multiplication
Chapter 3: Exponents

Guide 4B
Chapter 4: Counting
Chapter 5: Division
Chapter 6: Logic

Guide 4C
Chapter 7: Factors
Chapter 8: Fractions (+ & −)
Chapter 9: Integers

Guide 4D
Chapter 10: Fractions (× & ÷)
Chapter 11: Decimals
Chapter 12: Probability

Contents:

GrOk
Math lab
should probably hire
a bOdyguard
constantly
captured by

calamitous clOd
Almost always alliterates
Probably goOd at Juggling

Ms. Q.
Math Teacher

May someday turn
into a really big
butterfly

kraken
pirate shOp Teacher

kraken
Always keeps
an extra helmet handy,
Just in case

ROsencrantz and Guildenstern
custOdian(s?)
Have the same birthday!

when One eats,
does the Other
feel full?

FiOna
math team cOach
fastest 2-legged sprinter
in her grade at B.A.

The Headmaster
How to use this book

Welcome to Beast Academy!

This book is called the Guide.

There is also a separate Practice book with lots of problems you can use to sharpen your skills.

The Guide is written like a comic book.

In a comic book, whatever I say shows up in these bubbles. They're called comic balloons.

Here' one!

Each character has a different balloon color. This makes it easy to tell who is talking.

My balloons are purple!

The story is told in panels.

Panels usually h a rectangular fr around them..

...like this one.

Practice: Pages 6, 38, and 64

Contents: Chapter 4

See page 6 in the Practice book for a recommended reading/practice sequence for Chapter 4.

Chapter 4:
Counting

Good.

When you're counting the number of pages, you can't just subtract the first page number from the last.

$$\begin{array}{r} \cancel{84} \\ -\cancel{74} \\ \hline 10 \end{array}$$

For example, if you read pages 1 through 10, that's a total of 10 pages...

...not $10 - 1 = 9$ pages.

It's easy to count the number of pages you read if you start reading on page 1.

That's right. What could do to make the number of pages from 74 to 84 easier to count?

74	75	76	77	78	79	80	81	82	83	84
-73	-73	-73	-73	-73	-73	-73	-73	-73	-73	-73
1	2	3	4	5	6	7	8	9	10	11

We could subtract 73 from every page number!

That gives us a list of numbers from 1 to 11.

So, there are 11 pages.

eat! If you read pages 87 through 119, how many pages is that?

It will be easier to count the number of pages if we subtract 86 from every page number.

Why 86?

That way, the list of page numbers will start at 1!

How many pages are there from page 87 to page 119?

THE THREE DOTS ABOVE MEAN THAT SOME NUMBERS ARE NOT WRITTEN IN THE MIDDLE, BUT THE PATTERN CONTINUES.

INCLUDE MEANS TO KEEP IN. EXCLUDE MEANS TO LEAVE OUT.

To count the number of days from October 3rd to October 30th **inclusive**, we can subtract 2 from each date.

That gives us a list from 1 to 28, so there are 28 days to practice.

$$3 \quad 4 \quad 5 \quad \cdots \quad 28 \quad 29 \quad 30$$
$$-2 \quad -2 \quad -2 \quad \cdots \quad -2 \quad -2 \quad -2$$
$$1 \quad 2 \quad 3 \quad \cdots \quad 26 \quad 27 \quad 28$$

Perfect.

Now, let's find the number of days we have to practice from October 3rd to October 30th **exclusive**.

That means we **exclude** the 3rd and the 30th.

In that case, we start counting days on the 4th and stop on the 29th.

We subtract 3 from each date to get a list from 1 to 26.

So, if we don't include today, or the day of the math bowl, we only have 26 days to practice.

There's not much time! We better hit the books!

$$4 \quad 5 \quad 6 \quad \cdots \quad 27 \quad 28 \quad 29$$
$$-3 \quad -3 \quad -3 \quad \cdots \quad -3 \quad -3 \quad -3$$
$$1 \quad 2 \quad 3 \quad \cdots \quad 24 \quad 25 \quad 26$$

That's the spirit, Grogg! you read pages 74 to 84, solve the section review problems.

All of them?

The problems are numbered 1 through 55.

Try all of the even-numbered problems. We'll save the odd-numbered problems for later.

How many even-numbered problems are there?

Try it.

17

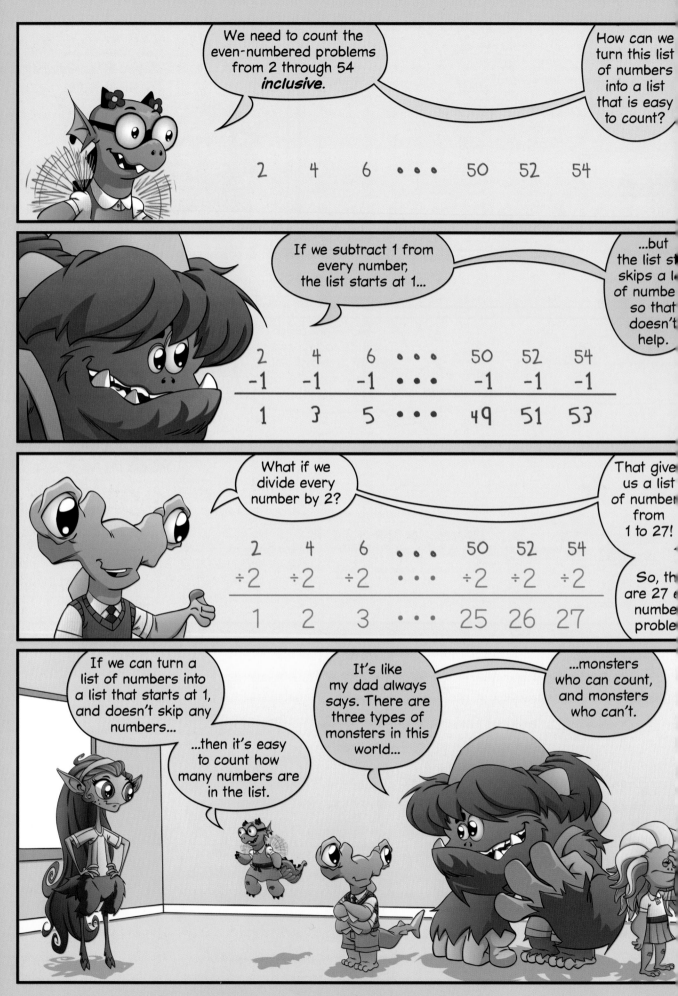

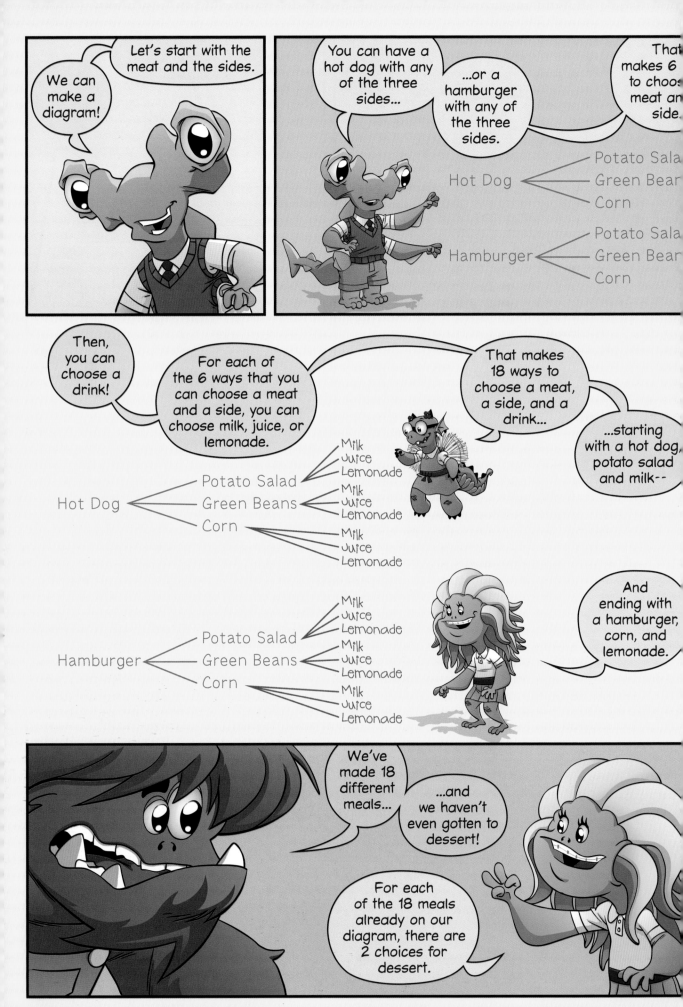

THIS IS CALLED A **TREE DIAGRAM**. IT IS USED FOR COUNTING POSSIBILITIES, LIKE THE NUMBER OF MEALS YOU CAN MAKE WITH THE GIVEN CHOICES.

What should R&G do?

23

I know! Some of the little monsters probably want mustard *and* ketchup!

Hmmm... How will that work?

We've added mustard to 20 hot dogs. We still have 5 plain hot dogs.

Let's set aside 1 of those for the monster who doesn't want mustard or ketchup.

Tha leaves hot dogs don't h musta

If we put ketchup on all 4 of these hot dogs, we still need ketchup on 9−4=5 more hot dogs.

We can put ketchup on 5 of the hot dogs that already have mustard!

That makes sense!

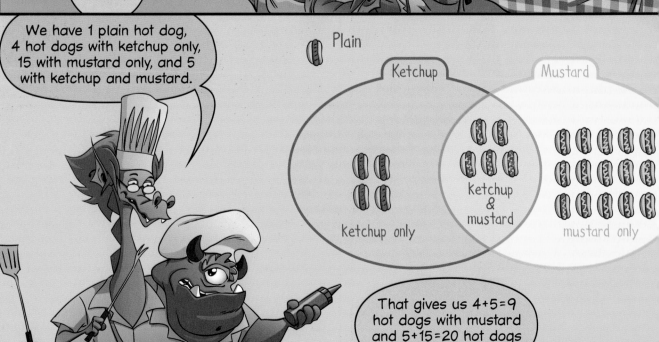

We have 1 plain hot dog, 4 hot dogs with ketchup only, 15 with mustard only, and 5 with ketchup and mustard.

Plain

Ketchup

Mustard

ketchup & mustard

Ketchup only

mustard only

That gives us 4+5=9 hot dogs with mustard and 5+15=20 hot dogs with ketchup.

THIS DIAGRAM IS CALLED A *VENN DIAGRAM*. EACH LABELED RING REPRESENTS A CATEGORY. THE ITEMS INSIDE EACH R BELONG IN THAT CATEGORY. ITEMS IN THE REGION WHERE THE TWO RINGS OVERLAP ARE PART OF BOTH CATEGORIES

ow for the mburgers.
How many hamburgers do we need to grill?
I'm not sure.
22 little monsters checked the box marked ketchup.
13 checked the box marked mustard.
And 3 didn't check either box.
hamburgers:
with ketchup: 22
with mustard: 13
plain(no k or m): 3
both(k & m): 7
But, 7 monsters checked both boxes.
't we just add numbers up to e out how many mburgers we eed to grill?
Nope.
Some of the little monsters got counted more than once.
For example, Lizzie checked ketchup and mustard on her form. I counted her as a monster who picked ketchup...
...a monster who picked mustard...
...and a monster who picked both.
Kiss the Cook
Maybe we should make another diagram.
Plain
Mustard
Ketchup
mustard only
mustard & Ketchup
Ketchup only
Use this diagram to help you figure out how many hamburgers must be grilled.

in

Mustard

Ketchup

mustard & Ketchup

mustard only

Ketchup only

We need 22 burgers with ketchup. Since 7 have mustard **and** ketchup...

...there must be 22−7=15 burgers with ketchup only.

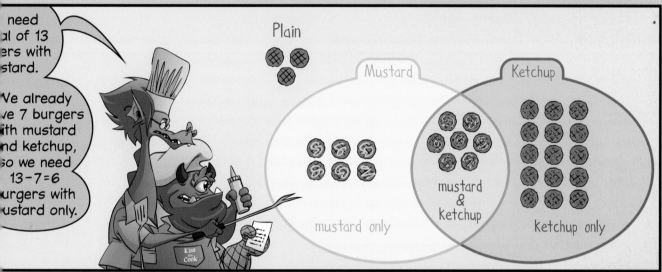

need
al of 13
ers with
stard.

We already
e 7 burgers
ith mustard
nd ketchup,
so we need
13−7=6
urgers with
ustard only.

Plain

Mustard

Ketchup

mustard only

mustard & ketchup

Ketchup only

makes 3 plain burgers,
rgers with mustard only,
h mustard and ketchup,
d 15 with ketchup only.

3+6+7+15=31 burgers we need to cook.

Plus this one I made for myself.

Want one?

No thanks, I'm a vegetarian.

27

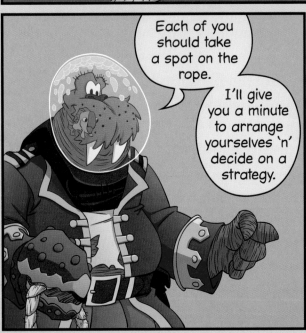

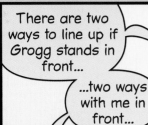

Excellent work, little monsters!

Four little monsters can line up in 4×3×2×1=24 ways on the rope.

There be a special shortcut for writin' 4×3×2×1.

We can put an exclamation point after a 4 to mean 4×3×2×1.

$$4! = 4 \times 3 \times 2$$

Four!

Arrr. Havin' an exclamation point after the 4 doesn't mean you *shout* the number...

...'tis called *4 factorial.*

Puttin' an exclamation point after a number tells you to multiply the number by each of the numbers below it...

...all the way down to 1.

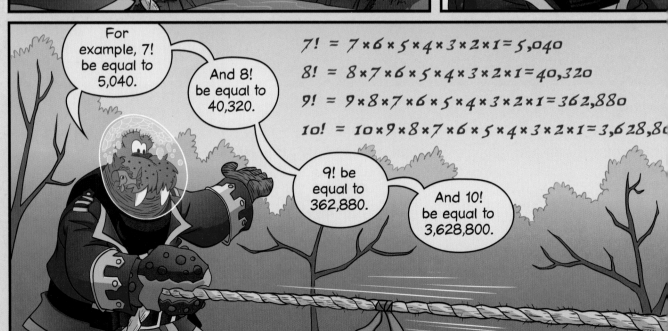

For example, 7! be equal to 5,040.

And 8! be equal to 40,320.

9! be equal to 362,880.

And 10! be equal to 3,628,800.

$$7! = 7 \times 6 \times 5 \times 4 \times 3 \times 2 \times 1 = 5,040$$
$$8! = 8 \times 7 \times 6 \times 5 \times 4 \times 3 \times 2 \times 1 = 40,320$$
$$9! = 9 \times 8 \times 7 \times 6 \times 5 \times 4 \times 3 \times 2 \times 1 = 362,880$$
$$10! = 10 \times 9 \times 8 \times 7 \times 6 \times 5 \times 4 \times 3 \times 2 \times 1 = 3,628,800$$

Those numbers get big fast!

20! = 2,432,902,008,176,640,000

Aye, 20 factorial be 2,432,902,008,176,640,000.

When would you ever use a factorial?

You just did!

When countin' the number o' ways to arrange 4 little monsters in order, you found 4!=4×3×2×1=24 ways.

We need another monster!

Plunk! Come play!

Shiver me timbers! That makes it five versus one.

How many different ways can the *five* of you little monsters arrange yourselves?

How many ways can the five little monsters arrange themselves?

33

There are 5 choices for the first monster, 4 choices for the second monster, 3 choices for the third, 2 choices for the fourth, and 1 choice for the last monster.

That makes $5 \times 4 \times 3 \times 2 \times 1 = 120$ ways to arrange five monsters!

$$5! = 5 \times 4 \times 3 \times 2 \times 1 = 1$$

$5 \times 4 \times 3 \times 2 \times 1$ is 5 factorial!

THE EXCLAMATION POINT NOTATION CAN BE CONFUSING. FOR EXAMPLE, IF ALEX SAYS "2 PLUS 3 IS 5!" HE MEANS 5, NOT $5 \times 4 \times 3 \times 2 \times 1$. WE WILL TRY TO MAKE IT CLEAR WHENEVER 5! MEANS 5 FACTORIAL.

Aye, 5 factorial gives us the number o' ways to arrange 5 little monsters in order.

Cammie! Come over to help!

With 6 little monsters, there are 6! ways to arrange ourselves.

$$6! = 6 \times (5 \times 4 \times 3 \times 2 \times 1)$$
$$= 6 \times 120$$
$$= 720$$

That's 720 ways!

Very good, little buccaneers.

Heave Ho!

SPLOSH

Practice: Pages 20-31

TITLE All of the 5!=120 ways to arrange 5 monsters in order:

NAME Alex

DATE 10/12

#	Code	#	Code	#	Code	#	Code
1.	GWALP	31.	WAGLP	61.	ALGWP	91.	LPGWA
2.	GWAPL	32.	WAGPL	62.	ALGPW	92.	LPGAW
3.	GWLAP	33.	WALGP	63.	ALWGP	93.	LPWGA
4.	GWLPA	34.	WALPG	64.	ALWPG	94.	LPWAG
5.	GWPAL	35.	WAPGL	65.	ALPGW	95.	LPAGW
6.	GWPLA	36.	WAPLG	66.	ALPWG	96.	LPAWG
7.	GAWLP	37.	WLGAP	67.	APGWL	97.	PGWAL
8.	GAWPL	38.	WLGPA	68.	APGLW	98.	PGWLA
9.	GALWP	39.	WLAGP	69.	APWGL	99.	PGAWL
10.	GALPW	40.	WLAPG	70.	APWLG	100.	PGALW
11.	GAPWL	41.	WLPGA	71.	APLGW	101.	PGLWA
12.	GAPLW	42.	WLPAG	72.	APLWG	102.	PGLAW
13.	GLWAP	43.	WPGAL	73.	LGWAP	103.	PWGAL
14.	GLWPA	44.	WPGLA	74.	LGWPA	104.	PWGLA
15.	GLAWP	45.	WPAGL	75.	LGAWP	105.	PWAGL
16.	GLAPW	46.	WPALG	76.	LGAPW	106.	PWALG
17.	GLPWA	47.	WPLGA	77.	LGPWA	107.	PWLGA
18.	GLPAW	48.	WPLAG	78.	LGPAW	108.	PWLAG
19.	GPWAL	49.	AGWLP	79.	LWGAP	109.	PAGWL
20.	GPWLA	50.	AGWPL	80.	LWGPA	110.	PAGLW
21.	GPAWL	51.	AGLWP	81.	LWAGP	111.	PAWGL
22.	GPALW	52.	AGLPW	82.	LWAPG	112.	PAWLG
23.	GPLWA	53.	AGPWL	83.	LWPGA	113.	PALGW
24.	GPLAW	54.	AGPLW	84.	LWPAG	114.	PALWG
25.	WGALP	55.	AWGLP	85.	LAGWP	115.	PLGWA
26.	WGAPL	56.	AWGPL	86.	LAGPW	116.	PLGAW
27.	WGLAP	57.	AWLGP	87.	LAWGP	117.	PLWGA
28.	WGLPA	58.	AWLPG	88.	LAWPG	118.	PLWAG
29.	WGPAL	59.	AWPGL	89.	LAPGW	119.	PLAGW
30.	WGPLA	60.	AWPLG	90.	LAPWG	120.	PLAWG

THE LAB

COUNTING PAIRS

Hi, little monsters.

Looks like you challenged Captain Kraken in tug-o-war.

Yep.

Maybe a g of badm will lift y spirits

Are you going to play against all *four* of us?

I only have three racquets...

...so I can only play against two little monsters at a time.

Who wants to play against Professor Grok first?

There must be at least ten different two-monster teams we can make.

Let's count them!

Splendid idea!

How many different 2-mons teams can you m from the four of little monsters

Ho d 2-mo are

...uld pair ...ith Alex, ...nie, or ...zzie.

GrOgg & Alex

That makes three possible teams that I am on.

GrOgg & Winnie

GrOgg & Lizzie

I could team up with Grogg, Winnie, or Lizzie.

Alex & Grogg

That makes three possible teams that I'm on.

Alex & Winnie

Alex & Lizzie

Winnie & Grogg

I could pair up with Grogg, Alex, or Lizzie.

Winnie & Alex

Winnie & Lizzie

I could ...up with ...g, Alex, ...Winnie.

Lizzie & Grogg

Each of the four of us can pair up with any of the other three. That makes a total of 4×3=12 possible teams.

Lizzie & Alex

Wait. Something is wrong.

Lizzie & Winnie

What's wrong?

Then, since I've already been paired with Frogg and Alex, there is only one monster left for me to pair up with.

Me!

G & A   A & W   A & L
G & W   A & L
G & L

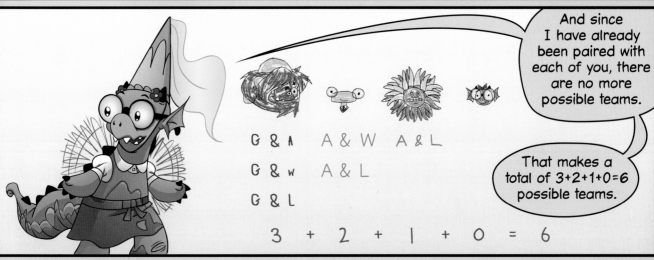

And since I have already been paired with each of you, there are no more possible teams.

That makes a total of 3+2+1+0=6 possible teams.

G & A   A & W   A & L
G & W   A & L
G & L

$$3 + 2 + 1 + 0 = 6$$

That's right! So, who would like to play first?

I will.

Me too.

Here comes the first serve!

If you beat me, I'll buy you each an ice cream.

Grok | Alex & Winnie
7 | 9

Grok
15

Grok | Alex & Winnie
19 | 21

Excellent form, little monsters.

Let's go get some ice cream.

You can each order a cup of vanilla ice cream with two toppings mixed in.

There are 20 different toppings to choose from!

And we each get to pick two.

Right.

Now, where is the proprietor of this establishment?

Ka-Flomp!

BWoRMp

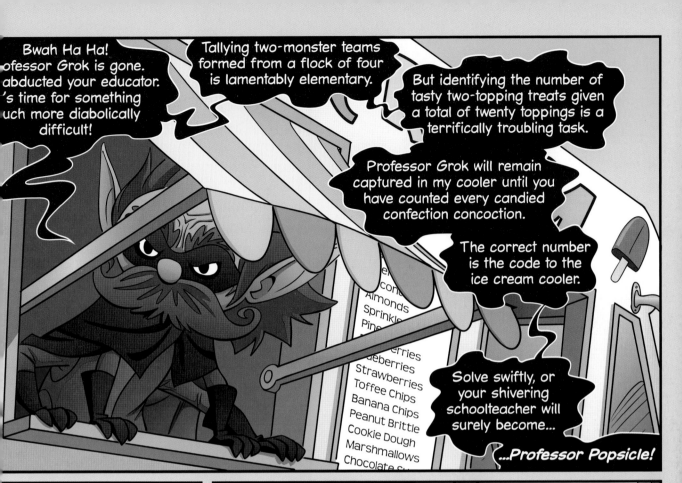

Bwah Ha Ha! Professor Grok is gone. I've abducted your educator. It's time for something much more diabolically difficult!

Tallying two-monster teams formed from a flock of four is lamentably elementary.

But identifying the number of tasty two-topping treats given a total of twenty toppings is a terrifically troubling task.

Professor Grok will remain captured in my cooler until you have counted every candied confection concoction.

The correct number is the code to the ice cream cooler.

Solve swiftly, or your shivering schoolteacher will surely become...

...Professor Popsicle!

There are twenty toppings!

How are we ever going to count every possible combination of two toppings?!

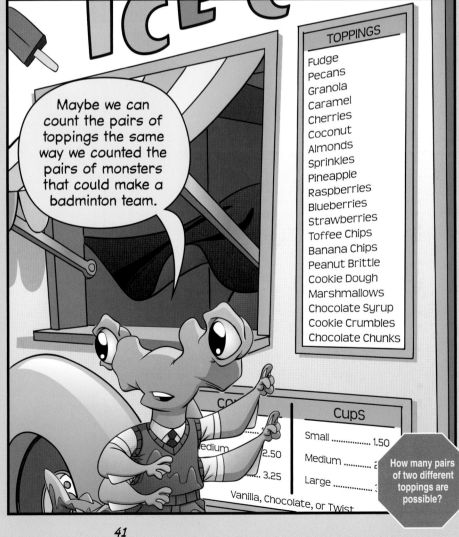

Maybe we can count the pairs of toppings the same way we counted the pairs of monsters that could make a badminton team.

TOPPINGS

Fudge
Pecans
Granola
Caramel
Cherries
Coconut
Almonds
Sprinkles
Pineapple
Raspberries
Blueberries
Strawberries
Toffee Chips
Banana Chips
Peanut Brittle
Cookie Dough
Marshmallows
Chocolate Syrup
Cookie Crumbles
Chocolate Chunks

CupS

Small 1.50
Medium 2
Large ....

Vanilla, Chocolate, or Twist

How many pairs of two different toppings are possible?

Starting with fudge... ...we can combine fudge with any of the other 19 toppings.

That gives us 19 different options.

Then, since pecans have already been paired with fudge... ...there are only 18 toppings left to pair with pecans.

That leaves 17 toppings to pair with granola.

If we pair each of the toppings with every topping below it, that will give us every possible pair of toppings.

We get 19+18+17+16+15+ +13+12+11+10+9+8 +6+5+4+3+2+1 pairs of toppings

TOPPINGS

Fudge 19
Pecans +18
Granola +17
Caramel +16
Cherries +15
Coconut +14
Almonds +13
Sprinkles +12
Pineapple +11
Raspberries +10
Blueberries +9
Strawberries +8
Toffee Chips +7
Banana Chips +6
Peanut Brittle +5
Cookie Dough +4
Marshmallows +3
Chocolate Syrup +2
Cookie Crumbles +1
Chocolate Chunks +

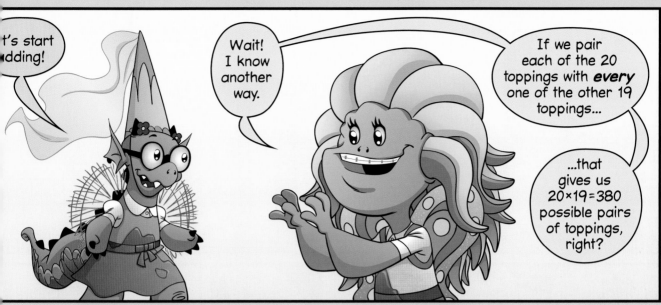

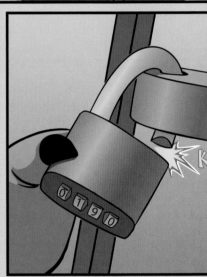

Lizzie

A quick way to add the numbers 1 through 19.
(Works for adding 1 through any number.)

$1 + 2 + 3 + 4 + 5 + 6 + 7 + 8 + 9 + 10 + 11 + 12 + 13 + 14 + 15 + 16 + 17 + 18 + 19$

If we copy the list of numbers forward and backward,
we can then add the list to itself:

$1 + 2 + 3 + 4 + 5 + 6 + 7 + 8 + 9 + 10 + 11 + 12 + 13 + 14 + 15 + 16 + 17 + 18 + 19$
$19 + 18 + 17 + 16 + 15 + 14 + 13 + 12 + 11 + 10 + 9 + 8 + 7 + 6 + 5 + 4 + 3 + 2 + 1$
$20+20+20+20+20+20+20+20+20+20+20+20+20+20+20+20+20+20+20$

This gives us nineteen 20's, which add up to $19 \times 20 = 380$.

But, since we added the list to itself, we have to divide
380 by 2 to find $1+2+3+4+5+ \cdots +16+17+18+19 = 380 \div 2 = 190$

So, to find the sum of the numbers
1 through 19, we can compute $19 \times 20 \div 2$.

This works for adding 1 through any number, like 1 to 100:

$1 + 2 + 3 + 4 + \cdots + 97 + 98 + 99 + 100$
$+ 100 + 99 + 98 + 97 + \cdots + 4 + 3 + 2 + 1$
$101 + 101 + 101 + 101 + \cdots + 101 + 101 + 101 + 101 = 100 \times 101 = 10,100$

Then, divide by 2: $10,100 \div 2 = 5,050$

Contents: Chapter 5

See page 38 in the Practice book for a recommended reading/practice sequence for Chapter 5.

Chapter 5:
Division

R & G
Special Quotients

Grogg, do you have your division homework?

I did it...

...but on one problem, I tried to divide by zero and my homework burst into flames.

I don' get i

Maybe we should try dividing by zero.

Alright, but we should go outside, just in case.

Agreed.

Let's try to divide six by zero.

We can use these pebbles.

All we need to do is split these six pebbles into *zero* piles.

?!?

?

48

We can't split six pebbles into *zero* piles.

Nope.

That doesn't make any sense.

There's more than one way to think about division. Maybe instead of making zero *piles*, we can make piles with zero *pebbles*.

Right, and we could see how many piles we can make.

?!?

That doesn't make any sense, either.

We can make as many piles of zero pebbles as we want.

And we'll *never* run out of pebbles!

I know! We can answer a division problem with multiplication.

Right!

To divide six by *three*, we could just answer, "What number times three is six?"

Perfect!

Two!

So, to divide six by *zero*, we need to answer, "What number times zero is six?"

???

Is there a number you can multiply by 6 to get 0?

49

Multiplying any number by zero gives you zero!

So there *isn't* a number that you can multiply by zero to get six!

You can't divide by zero. It doesn't make any sense!

DIVISION BY ZERO IS "UNDEFINED," WHICH IS ANOTHER WAY OF SAYING THAT IT DOESN'T MAKE ANY SENSE.

Let's try something else.

We can't divide six by zero.

Can we divide zero by six?

Let's see. If I have zer
pebbles, and I w
to place them i
6 cups...

...how r
pebb
will th
be
each c

That's easy! Each cup will have zero pebbles.

If we have zero pebbles, then no matter how many cups we try to place them into, we'll always end up with zero pebbles in each cup.

So zero divided by any number is zero except for 0÷0, which doesn't make sense.

Got

$0 \div n = 0$ FOR ALL NONZERO VALUES OF n.

ividing 1 is easy, too.

Don't tell me! I want to figure it out.

I'll start with 6÷1.

If I have 6 pebbles and I put them into one cup, the cup will contain all 6 pebbles...

...so 6÷1=6.

And no matter how many pebbles I start with, if I put them into just one cup, the cup will contain the same number I started with.

That's right!

Dividing any number by 1 gives you the same number you started with.

$n \div 1 = n$ FOR ALL VALUES OF n.

I know another one!

What do you get when you divide a number by itself?

Try it.

I'll try 6÷6.

If I divide 6 pebbles equally among 6 cups, there will be 1 pebble in each cup.

So, 6÷6=1.

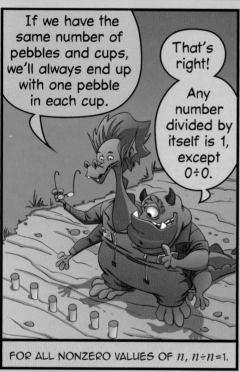

If we have the same number of pebbles and cups, we'll always end up with one pebble in each cup.

That's right! Any number divided by itself is 1, except 0÷0.

FOR ALL NONZERO VALUES OF n, $n÷n=1$.

This is a lot to remember. I better write these down.

If we divide a number by itself, we get--

1.

And any number divided by is--

The number.

Zero divided by anything is--

Zero.

Unless we try to divide by zero, which gives us--

Yikes!

Whoa!

Tho big pu monst was kiddi

How can we divide 3,500,00 by 7?

We can use multiplication to solve division problems!

Multiples of 10

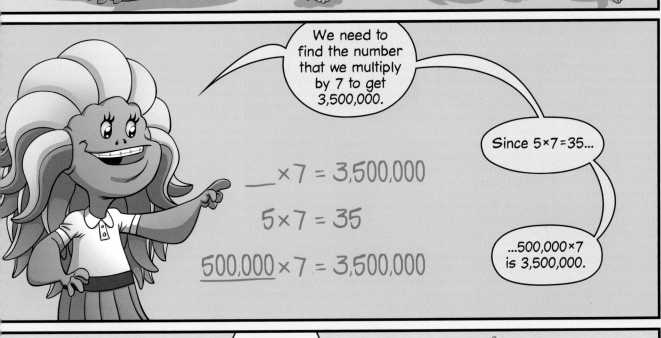

We need to find the number that we multiply by 7 to get 3,500,000.

Since 5×7=35...

...500,000×7 is 3,500,000.

$$\_\_ \times 7 = 3{,}500{,}000$$
$$5 \times 7 = 35$$
$$500{,}000 \times 7 = 3{,}500{,}000$$

So, 3,500,000÷7 =500,000!

Great job! Let's try another.

How can we divide 3,500 by 700?

$$\_\_ \times 7 = 3{,}500{,}000$$
$$5 \times 7 = 35$$
$$500{,}000 \times 7 = 3{,}500{,}000$$
$$3{,}500{,}000 \div 7 = 500{,}000$$

Try it.

We can just divide 36 thousands into groups of 9 thousands.

$36{,}000 \div 9{,}000$
$= 36 \div 9$
$= 4$

36 thousands divided into groups of 9 thousands gives us $36 \div 9 = 4$ groups!

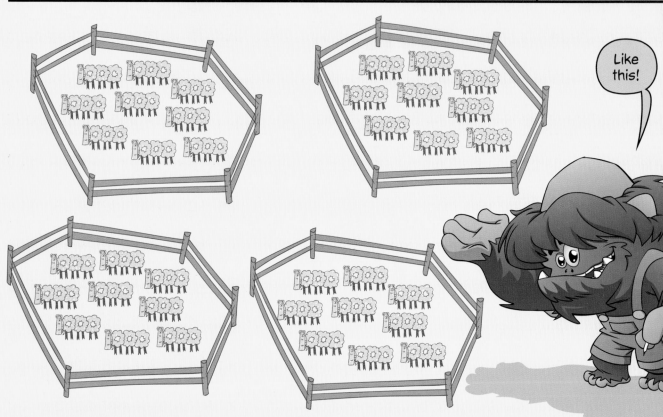

Like this!

Great thinking! Try this one. What is $6{,}000 \div 400$?

$6{,}000 \div 400$

6,000 is 6 **thousands**...

...but 400 is 4 **hundreds**.

I'm not su how we divi **thousand** into groups 4 **hundred**

How w you di 6,000÷

Instead of grouping 6,000 into **thousands**, and 400 into **hundreds**, maybe we can group both numbers the same way.

6 thousands is the same as **60** hundreds!

We can compute 6,000÷400 by dividing 60 **hundreds** into groups of 4 **hundreds!**

So, we can just divide 60÷4.

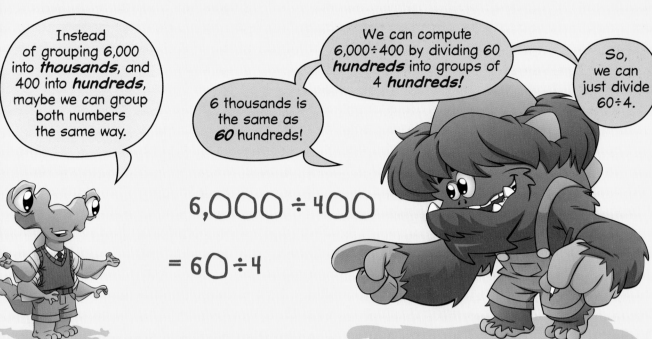

$$6,000 \div 400$$

$$= 6 \bigcirc \div 4$$

$$6,000 \div 400$$

$$= 6 \bigcirc \div 4$$

$$= 15$$

60 hundreds can be divided into 60÷4=15 groups of 4 hundreds.

So, 6,000÷400 equals 15!

Yep. That answer checks out.

$$15 \times 400 = 6,000$$

can remove the same number [of] zeros from the end of each [nu]mber in a division problem [wit]hout changing the quotient!

$$3,500 \div 700$$

$$= 35 \div 7$$

$$= 5$$

$$54,000 \div 6,000$$

$$= 54 \div 6$$

$$= 9$$

$$6,000 \div 400$$

$$= 60 \div 4$$

$$= 15$$

You're right, Winnie. Why does that work?

If both numbers in a division problem end in zero, then we can group both numbers into tens.

For example, 5,000 is 500 tens, and 200 is 20 tens.

So, dividing 5,000÷200 is the same as dividing 500 *tens* into groups of 20 *tens*.

$$5,000 \div 200$$
$$= 500 \div 20$$

So, 5,000÷200 =500÷20.

And dividing 500÷20 is the same as dividing 50 tens into groups of 2 tens.

So, 500÷20 =50÷2.

$$5,000 \div 200$$
$$= 500 \div 20$$
$$= 50 \div 2$$

I see. We can just keep removing a zero from each number until there are no more zeros to remove from one of the numbers.

Then, we divide.

$$5,000 \div 200$$
$$= 500 \div 20$$
$$= 50 \div 2$$
$$= 25$$

Very good. Removing the same number of zeros from the dividend and the divisor won't change the quotient.

Now, who can find this quotient?

$$15,000,000 \div 2,500,000$$

Tr

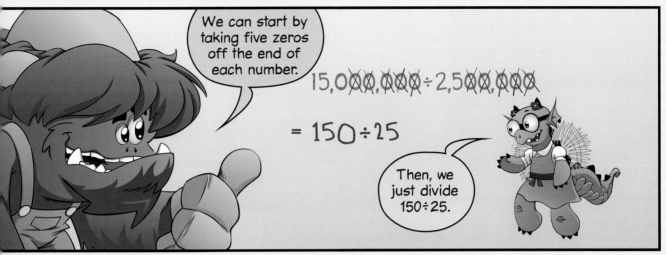

We can start by taking five zeros off the end of each number.

$$15,\!0\cancel{00},\!\cancel{000} \div 2,\!5\cancel{00},\!\cancel{000}$$

$$= 150 \div 25$$

Then, we just divide $150 \div 25$.

6 × 25 = 150, so 150 ÷ 25 = 6.

Superb!

Who can sum up what we've learned?

$$15,\!0\cancel{00},\!\cancel{000} \div 2,\!5\cancel{00},\!\cancel{000}$$

$$= 150 \div 25$$

$$= 6$$

If you want to be a division hero...

...all you have to do is drop the zeros.

Grogg, you're a poet.

You know it!

59

Practice: Pages 39-45

Workshop: LONG DIVISION

If 1,793 gold coins be divided among 32 pirates...

...how many coins be there in each pirate's share?

Since 1,800÷30 is 60, each pirate gets about 60 coins.

$$1793 \div 32$$
$$\approx 1800 \div 30$$
$$= 60$$

ESTIMATING AN ANSWER IS A GREAT FIRST STEP FOR MANY MATH PROBLEMS.

Aye. Good estimatin'...

...but how can we be findin' the *exact* number o' coins in each pirate's share?

If we start by giving 50 coins to each pirate...

...that's 32×50=1,600 coins.

That leave 1,793−1,600 coins to divid

each pirate gets:	coins left over:
50	1,793−1,600=193

Then, we can give each pirate at least 5 more coins, since 32×5=160.

That leaves 193−160=33 coins to divide.

So, each pirate can get one more coin.

That makes a total of 50+5+1=56 coins for each pirate...

...and coin le over

each pirate gets:	coins left over:
50	1,793−1,600 =193
+5	193−160 = 33
+1	33−32 = 1
56	1

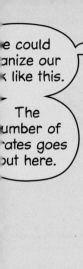

e could
anize our
k like this.

The
umber of
rates goes
ut here.

$$32\overline{)1{,}793}$$

And the number of coins goes here.

On top, we keep track of how many coins each pirate gets.

$$32\overline{)1{,}793}$$

And down here, we keep track of how many coins are left over.

We can give each pirate at least 50 coins.

$$\begin{array}{r} 50 \\ 32\overline{)1{,}793} \\ -1{,}600 \\ \hline 193 \end{array}$$

After we subtract 32×50=1,600 from 1,793...

...there are 193 coins left to divide.

Then, we can ive each pirate 5 more coins.

$$\begin{array}{r} 5 \\ 50 \\ 32\overline{)1{,}793} \\ -1{,}600 \\ \hline 193 \\ -160 \\ \hline 33 \end{array}$$

e subtract
2×5=160
rom 193.

And we have 33 coins left to divide.

Finally, we can give each pirate one more coin.

That makes 56 coins for each pirate.

$$\begin{array}{r} 1 \\ 5 \\ 50 \end{array}\Big\}56$$

$$\begin{array}{r} 32\overline{)1{,}793} \\ -1{,}600 \\ \hline 193 \\ -160 \\ \hline 33 \\ -32 \\ \hline 1 \end{array}$$

And one coin left over.

WE SAY THAT 1,793÷32 HAS QUOTIENT 56 AND REMAINDER 1.

Aye. Excellent figurin'. Try another.

If 7,972 coins be divided among 24 pirates...

...how many coins be there in each pirate's share?

Try

To start, we can give 200 coins to each pirate.

That's 24×200=4,800 coins. So, there are 3,172 coins left over.

$$
\begin{array}{r}
100 \\
200 \\
24\overline{)7{,}972} \\
-4{,}800 \\
\hline
3{,}172 \\
-2{,}400 \\
\hline
772
\end{array}
$$

Then, we give 100 more to each pirate, which leaves 3,172−2,400=772 coins to divide.

We give each pirate 20 more, then 10 more, and finally 2 more coins...

...for a total of 200+100+20+10+2 =332 coins each, with 4 left over.

$$
\begin{array}{r}
2 \\
10 \\
20 \\
100 \\
200
\end{array}\Bigg\} 332
$$

$$
\begin{array}{r}
24\overline{)7{,}972} \\
-4{,}800 \\
\hline
3{,}172 \\
-2{,}400 \\
\hline
772 \\
-480 \\
\hline
292 \\
-240 \\
\hline
52 \\
-48 \\
\hline
4
\end{array}
$$

My work looks completely different, but I got the same answer.

Me, too.

Same here.

Arrr.... Let's have a look at your work, little monsters.

Aye. To avoid arithmetic errors, 'tis good to choose numbers that be easy to multiply by 24.

This usually means choosin' multiples of th' powers o' 10.

Like 10, 30, or 200.

That's why I used 100.

Because 100×24 is easy to compute.

'Tis also a good idea to limit the number o' steps ye be takin'.

That's why I started with 300. It's not quite as easy to multiply by 24 as 100 is.

But, I didn't need to take as many steps as Alex.

Aye. Fewer steps means fewer chances to make mistakes.

My mom says that every mistake is an opportunity!

She also says that I've had **way** more opportunities than most little monsters my age.

For last night's homework, I figured out 36,063÷9...

...in my *head!*

In your head?

Yep.

Whoa. How?

I made it a problem about donuts, like I often do with division problems.

Huh?

ou see, ave 36,063 s to divide lly among monsters...

don't divide all at ce.

RANDY'S DONUTS
10 mi.

I start by dividing 36,000 donuts.

Then, I divide the other 63.

Because 36,000 and 63 are both easy to divide by 9!

Exactly.

Try to compute 36,063÷9 in your head.

If I divide 36,000 donuts between 9 monsters, each monster gets 36,000÷9=4,000 donuts.

Then, when you divide the remaining 63 donuts...

...each monster gets 63÷9=7 more donuts.

That makes a total of 4,000+7=4,007 donuts for each monster.

Good thinking, Grogg!

Some numbers are easiest to divide one part at a time.

There's only one problem with using donuts to solve division problems.

Now I'm starving for a donut!

Oh yeah? What's that?

Multiples of 5 end in 0 or 5.

$5 \times 0 = 0$
$5 \times 1 = 5$
$5 \times 2 = 10$
$5 \times 3 = 15$
$5 \times 4 = 20$
$5 \times 5 = 25$
$5 \times 6 = 30$
$5 \times 7 = 35$

Any number that is divisible by 5 ends in 0 or 5.

Is **every** number that ends in 0 or 5 divisible by 5?

Huh?

What if someone told you that 5,393,680 is **not** divisible by 5.

How could you convince them that 5,393,680 **is** divisible by 5?

5,393,680

Are you sure that 5,393,680 is divisible by 5?

We know that 5,393,680 is a multiple of 10, since it ends in zero.

$539,368 \times 10 = 5,393,680.$

$5,393,680 = 10 \times 539,368$

Since =10... ...we know that $(5 \times 2) \times 539,368 = 5,393,680.$

5,393,680 is 5 times $(2 \times 539,368)$.

So, 5,393,680 is definitely a multiple of 5!

Since $2 \times 5 = 10$, every multiple of 10 is a multiple of 5.

So, any number that ends in 0 is divisible by 5.

$$5,393,680 = 10 \times 539,368$$
$$= (5 \times 2) \times 539,368$$
$$= 5 \times (2 \times 539,368)$$

Very good.

How could you convince me that 76,345 is divisible by 5?

Since 76,340 is a multiple of 5...

...adding 5 more gives the next mult of 5, which 76,345.

So, 76,345 is definitely divisible by 5.

Every number that ends in 5 is five more than a number that ends in 0.

And since every number that ends in 0 is a multiple of 5, every number that ends in 5 is a multiple of 5.

So, every number that ends in 0 or 5 is divisible by 5.

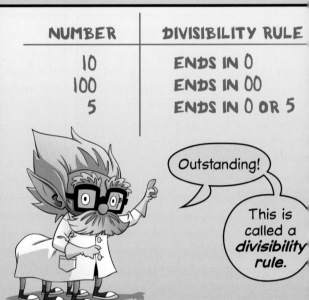

NUMBER	DIVISIBILITY RULE
10	ENDS IN 0
100	ENDS IN 00
5	ENDS IN 0 OR 5

Outstanding!

This is called a **divisibility rule**.

Are there divisibility rules for other numbers?

Indeed!

For example, there is a quick way to tell whether or not a number is divisible by 25.

Can you tell which of these numbers is divisible by 25?

7,841,955
7,841,965
7,841,975
7,841,985

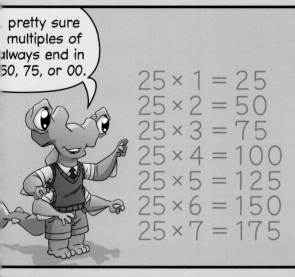

pretty sure multiples of ...lways end in ...0, 75, or 00.

$$25 \times 1 = 25$$
$$25 \times 2 = 50$$
$$25 \times 3 = 75$$
$$25 \times 4 = 100$$
$$25 \times 5 = 125$$
$$25 \times 6 = 150$$
$$25 \times 7 = 175$$

So, 7,841,975 is divisible by 25!

7,841,955
7,841,965
(7,841,975)
7,841,985

...How ... you be ...letely sure ... 7,841,975 ...visible by 25?

We know that 7,841,900 is a multiple of 100, since it ends in 00.

And since 100=25×4, every multiple of 100 is also a multiple of 25!

$$7{,}841{,}900 = 100 \times 78{,}419$$
$$= (25 \times 4) \times 78{,}419$$
$$= 25 \times (4 \times 78{,}419)$$

...ce 7,841,900 is a ...ple of 25, we can ... 25's to 7,841,900 ...ind the next few ...ultiples of 25.

7,841,975 is a multiple of 25, so it's divisible by 25.

7,841,900 ⎫ +25
7,841,925 ⎫ +25
7,841,950 ⎫ +25
7,841,975

To see if a ...umber is divisible ... 25, we only need ... look at its last two digits.

If the last two digits of a number are 00, 25, 50, or 75...

...then the ...umber is ...ivisible by 25.

NUMBER	DIVISIBILITY RULE
10	ENDS IN 0
	ENDS IN 00
	ENDS IN 0 OR 5
	ENDS...

Very good! Let's add that rule to our list.

Since we know that 1,112,200 is divisible by 4...

...we can count up by 4's to get the next few multiples of 4.

1,112,200 ⟩ +4
1,112,204 ⟩ +4
1,112,208 ⟩ +4
1,112,212 ⟩ +4
1,112,216 ⟩ +4
1,112,220 ⟩ +4
1,112,224

We skip right over 1,112,222.

So, 1,112,222 is *not* a multiple of 4.

How ab 5,523,2

7,762,323
1,112,222
5,523,278
5,552,368
8,675,309

5,523,200 is divisible by 4.

We can count by 4's to see if 5,523,278 is a multiple of 4.

5,523,200 ⟩ +4
5,523,204 ⟩ +4
5,523,208 ⟩ +4
5,523,212 ⟩ +4
5,523,216 ⟩ +4
5,523,220 ⟩
5,523,

Wait, Alex. You don't need to write the whole numbers.

Just write the last two digits.

5,52
5,5
5,52
5,523,212 ⟩ +4
5,523,216 ⟩ +4
523,220 ⟩ +4
523,224 ⟩ +4
523,228 ⟩ +4
523,232
36 ⟩
40

Since we start at 00 and add 4's--

The last 2 digits make multiples of 4.

5,523,200 +4
5,523,204 +4
5,523,208 +4
5,523,212 +4
523,216 +4
23,220 +4
523,224 +4
523,228 +4
523,232 +4
36 ⟩
40

You'll eventually get up to 5,523,2**80**, but you'll skip right over 5,523,2**78**.

72 ⟩
76 ⟩
80 ⟩

Since 78 isn't a multip of 4, neither 5,523,2**78**.

74

Practice: Pages 56-63

Contents: Chapter 6

See page 64 in the Practice book for a recommended reading/practice sequence for Chapter 6.

Chapter 6:
Logic

R&G Logic Puzzles

What are we doing at the docks?

Captain Kraken wants us to load this luggage onto his ship.

He's taking some little monsters on an overnight field trip.

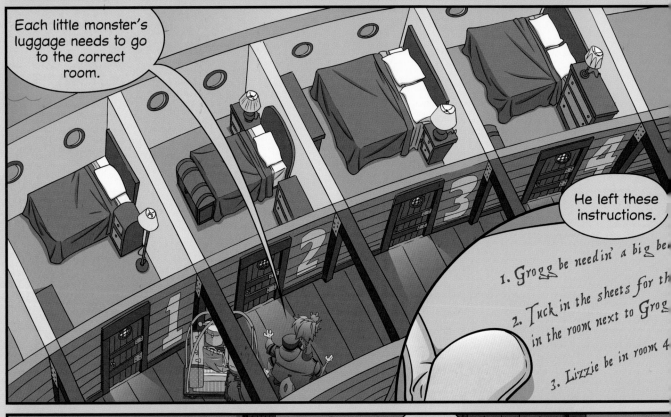

Each little monster's luggage needs to go to the correct room.

He left these instructions.

1. Grogg be needin' a big be...

2. Tuck in the sheets for th... in the room next to Grog...

3. Lizzie be in room 4

It's a logic puzzle!

We can use these clues to figure out which room each little monster is in.

I'll show you!

We've got just enough time for one more practice before we arrive at the site of this year's regional Math Bowl.

A lot of the problems you'll see in the Math Bowl will be more like puzzles than math problems.

Here's an example.

In this Sudoku puzzle, a 4×4 grid is separated into four smaller 2×2 grids, called **boxes**.

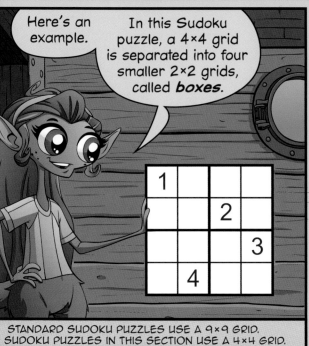

STANDARD SUDOKU PUZZLES USE A 9×9 GRID.
SUDOKU PUZZLES IN THIS SECTION USE A 4×4 GRID.

The goal is to place a digit in each small square so that every row, column, and box in the grid contains each of the digits 1 through 4, like this.

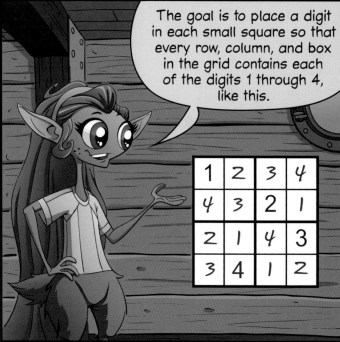

Try this one.

Where do we begin?

Great question! Figuring out where to start a puzzle is a very important step.

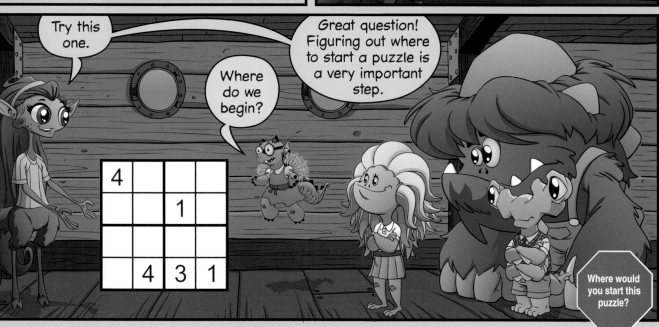

Where would you start this puzzle?

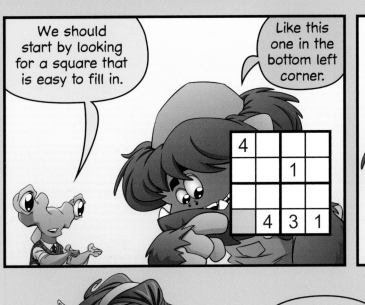

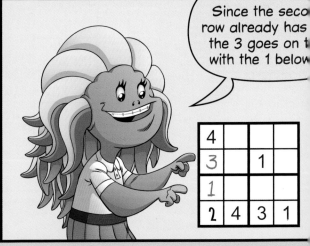
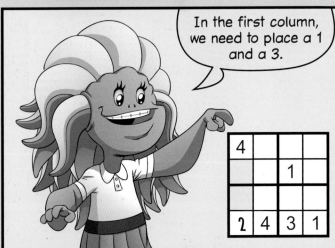

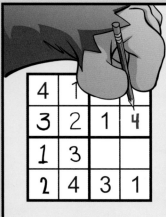

"Nice work."

"Solving these puzzles doesn't require any special knowledge, just careful thought."

"We call this *logical reasoning*."

"Here's a similar type of puzzle."

"As in the first puzzle, we begin with a 4×4 grid."

"The goal is to place a digit in each small square so that every row and column contains each of the digits 1 through 4."

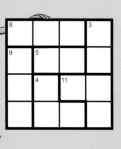

"However, this time the grid is split into regions, called *cages*."

"Each cage contains a small number that gives the sum of the digits in the cage."

4 + 2 + 3 = 9

"Try this one."

Try it.

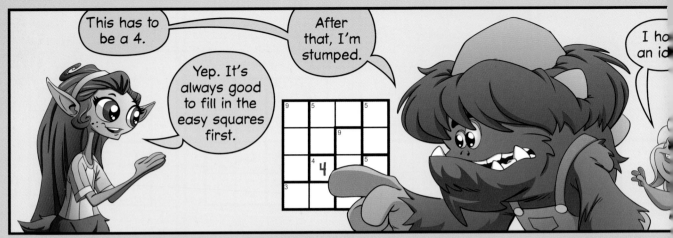

This has to be a 4.

Yep. It's always good to fill in the easy squares first.

After that, I'm stumped.

I ho... an id...

Since every row and column has a 1, a 2, a 3, and a 4...

...the sum of the numbers in any row or column is always 1+2+3+4=10.

How does that help?

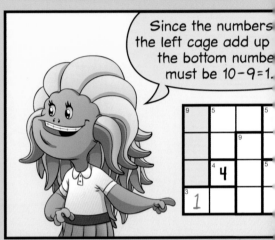

Since the numbers the left cage add up the bottom numbe must be 10−9=1.

We can do the same thing here.

That means this number must be a 2, since 1+2=3.

Next, since this column already has a 4 and a 2, these squares contain a 1 and a 3.

The top row already has a 1, so the 3 goes on top, with the 1 below it.

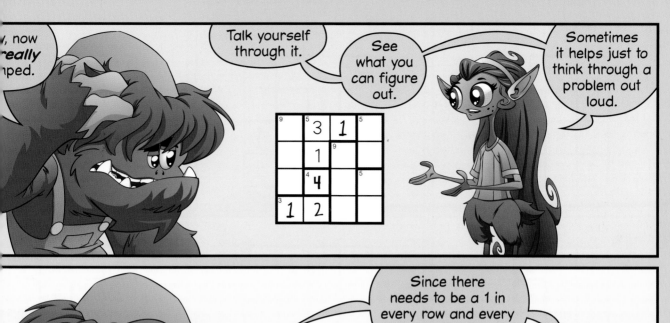

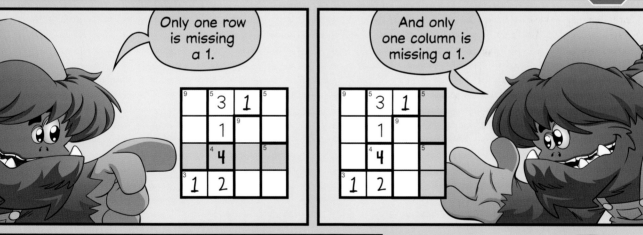

Code Breaker

Game Play:

Code Breaker is a pencil-and-paper game for two players, a coder and a guesser. The coder secretly chooses three different digits to make a 3-digit code. The guesser tries to guess the code. After each guess, the coder gives two clues:
- How many of the digits in the guess are correct.
- How many of the correct digits are in the right place.

The guesser tries to guess the code in as few tries as possible.
Each guess must be a 3-digit code whose digits are all different.
The guesser keeps track of guesses and clues as shown below.

Guess	Correct Digits	Right Place
123	0	0
456	1	0
789	1	1
580	1	0
704	2	0
049	3	3 yay!

If you want to keep score, take turns as coder and guesser.
Award 1 point to the coder for each incorrect guess, and 10 points to the guesser for a correct guess.

Variations:

You can play Code Breaker with 4-digit numbers.
Each player can have a code. In this case, players take turns trying to guess the other player's code, with clues given after each guess. The first player to correctly guess the other player's code wins. Take turns guessing first.

Code Breaker is a slight variation of a game called Bulls and Cows.
The game Mastermind is also very similar, but uses colored pegs instead of digits.

Sample Game:
Grogg chooses 049 as his secret code.

Winnie's first guess is 123. Grogg tells Winnie that she has 0 correct digits, and 0 digits in the correct place.

Winnie guesses 456 next. Grogg tells Winnie that she has 1 correct digit, and 0 digits in the correct place.

Winnie guesses 789. Grogg tells Winnie that she has 1 correct digit, and 1 digit in the correct place.

Winnie guesses 580. Grogg tells Winnie that she has 1 correct digit, and 0 digits in the correct place.

Winnie guesses 704. Grogg tells Winnie that she has 2 correct digits, and 0 digits in the correct place.

Winnie uses the 5 clues above to figure out Grogg's code, 049!

THE LAB
TRUTH & LIES

Arrr. This be as far as I can take you.

Aren't you coming with us?

I'll be tendin' to me ship, but I'll be here when you get back.

Have fun!

You guys go on ahead. Professor Grok waiting for you the dock.

Professor Grok! How did you get here?

I rode my armadactyl.

Inconceivable!

Do you know how to get to the Math Bowl?

No, but I'm sure we'll be able to find it just by asking some of the locals.

There's just one problem.

What's that?

Some of the monsters on this island *always* tell the truth, but the rest *always* lie.

How can you tell the liars from the truth-tellers?

You ask them questions.

Pardon me. Are you a liar?

No.

See, Winnie. That was easy!

Grogg! Whether he is a liar or a truth-teller, his answer will always be "No."

If he's a liar, he'll lie and say he's not a liar.

And if he's a truth-teller, he'll tell the truth and say he's not a liar.

So, we don't know if he was lying, or telling the truth.

Oh, right. ...ess we need ...k a different ...question.

I've got one!

How many arms do I have?

7.

CREATING A TABLE THAT LISTS ALL THE POSSIBILITIES IS OFTEN A GREAT WAY TO SOLVE PROBLEMS LIKE THESE.

Okay... We've finished almost all of the problems.

We've got about 10 minutes to do the two we haven't solved yet.

Number 13 is reeeealy confusing.

Question 13

Two purple hats and three orange hats are placed in a bag. Anna, Bridget, and Clara are all blindfolded. Each pulls a hat from the bag and puts it on her own head. When the blindfolds are removed, each girl can see the hats on the other girls, but not her own hat. Professor Pickle asks Anna, "Do you know what color your hat is?" Anna says, "No." Professor Pickle then asks Bridget, "Do you know the color of your hat?" Bridget says, "I didn't know before Anna said 'no', but now I do."
What color is the hat on each girl's head?

Anna_____ Bridget_____ Clara_____

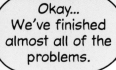

Rea
the pro
carefu
twic

If Anna doesn't know the color of her own hat, how are **we** supposed to figure it out?

How **could** Anna know the color of her own hat?

She ca
only se
Bridget'
and Clar
hats.

What woul
Anna need
see in order
know her ow
color?

SUMMARY: 1. BRIDGET AND CLARA DON'T BOTH HAVE PURPLE HATS 2. ANNA AND CLARA DON'T BOTH HAVE PURPLE HATS.

Unless Clara's hat is purple!*

Exactly! Bridget **knows** that Anna doesn't see **two** purple hats.

So, if Bridget sees a **purple** ha[t] on Clara, then Brid[get] knows that her own [hat] **cannot** be purple[, it] has to be orange[.]

*IF BRIDGET SEES AN ORANGE HAT ON CLARA, BRIDGET HAS NO WAY OF KNOWING THE COLOR OF HER OWN HAT, BECAU[SE] BRIDGET DOESN'T KNOW WHETHER ANNA SAW TWO ORANGE HATS, OR AN ORANGE HAT AND A PURPLE HAT.

So, Clara has a purple hat, and Bridget has an orange hat.

And since Bridget doesn't see two purple hats, Anna's hat is orange, too.

Got it!

Two purple hats and three orange hats are placed in a bag. Anna, Bridget, and Clara are all blindfolded. Each pulls a hat from the bag and puts it on her own head. When the blindfolds are removed, each girl can see the hats on the other girls, but not her own hat. Professor Pickle asks Anna, "Do you know what color your hat is?" Anna says, "No." Professor Pickle then asks Bridget, "Do you know the color of your hat?" Bridget says, "I didn't know before Anna said 'no', but now I do."
What color is the hat on each girl's head?

Anna _Orange_   Bridget _Orange_   Clara _Purple_

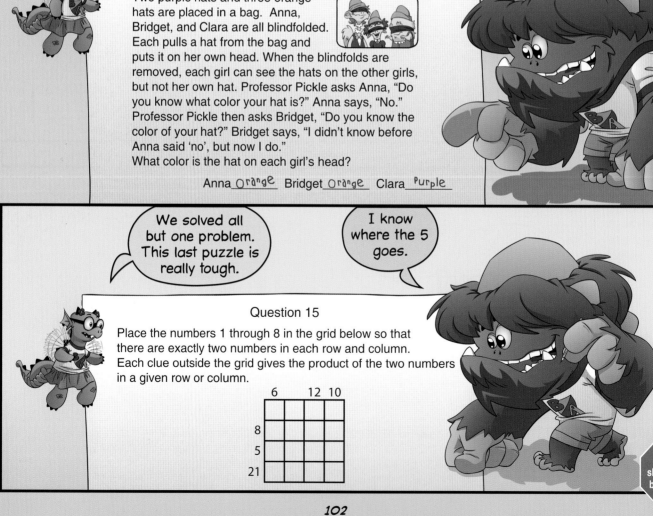

We solved all but one problem. This last puzzle is really tough.

I know where the 5 goes.

Question 15

Place the numbers 1 through 8 in the grid below so that there are exactly two numbers in each row and column.
Each clue outside the grid gives the product of the two numbers in a given row or column.

```
      6    12  10
   +---+---+---+---+
 8 |   |   |   |   |
   +---+---+---+---+
 5 |   |   |   |   |
   +---+---+---+---+
21 |   |   |   |   |
   +---+---+---+---+
```

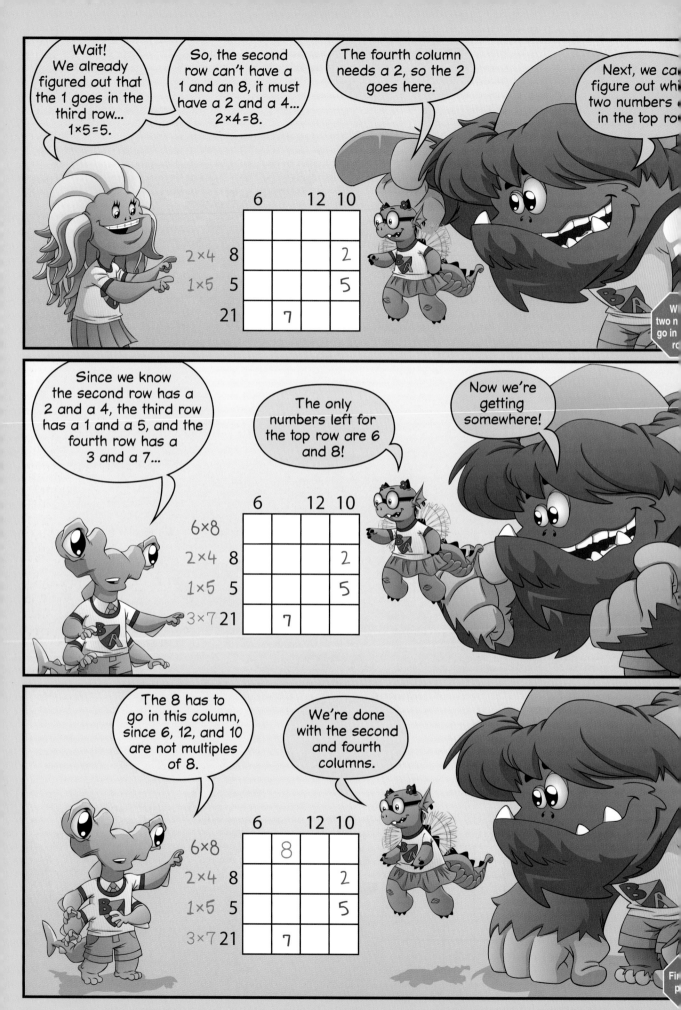

That Max kid really clobbered us.

He was so fast!

He knew most of the answers befo I even finishe reading the questions!

2nd place. Pretty good for our first try!

Index

For additional books,
printables, and more, visit
www.BeastAcademy.com